The Sunday Worship Duet Book

Hymns, Classics, and Songs of Praise

Arranged by

Tom Fettke

LILLENAS PUBLISHING COMPANY
Kansas City, MO 64141

CONTENTS

Praise to the Lord, the Almighty

with

Praise God, from Whom All Blessings Flow

Arr. by Tom Fettke

*"Praise God, from Whom All Blessings Flow" (Thomas Ken - Louis Bourgeois)

4

Him a-bove, ye heav'n-ly host. Praise Fa-ther, Son, and Ho - ly

Ghost.

CD1:02

Faster ♩ = ca. 128

Faster

*"Praise to the Lord, the Almighty" (Joachim Neander - *Stralsund Gesangbuch, 1665*)

Solo or both voices continue unison

Praise to the Lord, the Al - might-y, the King of cre - a - tion!

O my soul, praise Him, for He is thy health and sal - va - tion!

6

8

My Jesus, I Love Thee

WILLIAM R. FEATHERSTON

DEBORAH CRISER
Duet arr. by Tom Fettke

My Je-sus, I love Thee; I know Thou art mine.

For Thee all the fol - lies of sin I re - sign.

12

crown on my brow, "If ev-er I loved Thee, my Je - sus, 'tis now." "If ev-er I loved Thee, my Je - sus, 'tis now."

His Eye Is on the Sparrow

MRS. C. D. MARTIN

CHARLES H. GABRIEL
Arr. by Tom Fettke

18

*Or (4) if you are counting 2 beats per measure.

I Want to Be Like Jesus

with

Lord, Be Glorified

Arr. by Tom Fettke

**Cued notes optional. Measures 7 through 10 may be more effective singing unison melody.

23

*"I Want to Be Like Jesus" (Thomas Chisholm-David Ives)

Lyrics:
I have one deep, supreme desire– That I may be like Jesus. To this I fervently aspire– That I may be like Jesus. I want my heart His throne to be, So that a watching world may see

*Copyright © 1945, renewed 1973, arr. © 1993 by Lillenas Publishing Co (SESAC). All rights reserved.
Administered by The Copyright Company, 40 Music Square East, Nashville, TN 37203.

24

Sing Hallelujah

J. H.

JACK HAYFORD
Arr. by Tom Fettke

1st verse: unison melody (Voice II)
2nd verse: parts

Voice I (high)

1. There has not failed one word of all His prom - ise;
2. Whirl - winds of change are blow - ing 'cross the na - tions;

Voice II (low)

1. There has not failed one word of all His prom - ise;
2. Whirl - winds of change are blow - ing 'cross the na - tions;

28

seek to steal your joy. Hear Je - sus speak, "I've prayed for you; you'll_ fail not." And sing hal - le - lu - jah! I am o - ver - com - ing!

When in the fi - 'ry fur - nace of af - flic - tion

Chil - dren of light, the dark - ness fast is gath - 'ring.

Earth's black - est mid - night comes; its last trav - ail be -

gins. Stand in the light– God's

Word out - shines the__ shad - ows; Sing hal - le -

Be Thou My Vision

TRADITIONAL IRISH HYMN
Translated by Mary E. Byrne
Versified by Eleanor H. Hull

TRADITIONAL IRISH MELODY
Arr. by Tom Fettke

Heart of my own heart, what-ev-er be-fall,

Still be my Vi-sion, O Rul-er of all.

Be Thou my Vi-sion, O Lord of my heart.

Shine, Jesus, Shine

G. K.

GRAHAM KENDRICK
Arr. by Tom Fettke

Set us free by the truth You now bring us. Shine on
Search me, try me, con - sume all my dark - ness. Shine on

me, shine on me.
me, shine on

Shine, Je - sus, shine;—— fill this land—— with the Fa - ther's glo - ry.

Blaze, Spir - it, blaze;—— set out hearts on—— fire.

Flow, riv - er, flow;___ flood the na - tions with grace and mer - cy.

Send forth Your Word,___ Lord, and let___ there be light.___

D.S. al Coda ⊕ CODA

me.___

3. As we gaze on Your king - ly bright - ness, So our fac - es dis-

play Your like - ness. Ev - er chang - ing from glo - ry to glo - ry,

Mir - rored here, may our lives tell Your sto - ry. Shine on ____

me, _____ shine on ____ me. _____

Shine, Je - sus, shine; ____ fill this land ____ with the Fa - ther's glo - ry.

CD1:26

Blaze, Spir - it, blaze;___ set our hearts on___ fire.___

Flow, riv - er, flow;___ flood the na - tions with grace and mer - cy.

Send forth Your Word,___ Lord, and let___ there be light.

Let there be light. Shine, Je - sus, shine!___

Use two lowest notes if range is too high.

He Takes Away the Sins of the World

KEN BIBLE and PHILIP P. BLISS

TOM FETTKE and PHILIP P. BLISS
Arr. by Tom Fettke

slight rit.   sub. *mp*   (55) a tempo

Can it be? He takes a-way the sins of the

slight rit.   *sub.mp* a tempo

CD1:30

cresc. poco a poco   accel.

world.

cresc. poco a poco   accel.

(60) Faster ♩ = ca. 76

f

When He comes, our glo - rious King, All His ran - somed

Faster

f

(64) cresc.

home to bring, Then a - new this song we'll sing, "Hal - le -

cresc.

Praise, My Soul, the King of Heaven

HENRY F. LYTE

MARK ANDREWS
Arr. by Tom Fettke

51

52

Res - cues us___ from all our foes.

Duet (or continue solo)

Al - le - lu - ia! Al - le - lu - ia!

Wide - ly yet His mer - cy flows.___

CD1:33

54

Shining Light

includes
Find Us Faithful
Song for the Nations

Arr. by Tom Fettke

shin - ing light to the peo - ples of the earth, Till the whole world sees the

cresc.

glo - ry of Your name. May Your pure light shine through us.

Voice I *mf*

Voice II

May we bring a word of hope to the na - tions, A

(27) Slightly faster ♩ = ca. 72

Mel.

Slightly faster

(31)

word of life to the peo - ples of the earth, Till the whole world knows there's sal-

CD1:37

61

CD1:38

When I Survey

ISAAC WATTS

LOWELL MASON and TOM FETTKE
Arr. by Tom Fettke

For - bid it, Lord, that____ I should____ boast,

Save in the death of____ Christ, my____ God.

All the vain things that____ charm me____ most,

I sac - ri - fice them____ to His____ blood.

68

The Honors of Thy Name

includes

O for a Thousand Tongues to Sing
Blessed Be the Name

Arr. by Tom Fettke

CD1:44 With great intensity ♩ = ca. 92

mp cresc. poco a poco

5

*"O for a Thousand Tongues to Sing" (Charles Wesley-Carl Glazer)

Voice I (high) *f* 9

Voice II (low)

Hear Him, ye deaf; His praise, ye dumb, Your loos-ened tongues em-

f

13

ploy; Ye__ blind, be-hold your__ Sav-ior come; And__ leap, ye lame, for

rit.

71

*"Blessed Be the Name" (Stanzas, Charles Wesley; Refrain, Ralph Hudson - Music Anonymous)

74

76

Holy, Holy, Holy

with

Holy Is the Lord of Hosts

Arr. by Tom Fettke

*"Holy, Holy, Holy" (Reginald Heber - John B. Dykes)

*"Holy, Holy, Holy" (Reginald Heber - Tom Fettke)

*"Holy Is the Lord of Hosts" (Nolene Prince)

glo - ry, The whole earth is full of His glo - ry, The

whole earth is full of His glo - ry; Ho - ly is the

Lord! Ho - ly is the

Lord. A - men!

Use cue notes if higher ending is desirable

With Wings as Eagles

PAUL WILLIAMS
Adapted from Isaiah 40:28-31; Habakkuk 3:17-18

BENJAMIN HARLAN
Duet arr. by Tom Fettke

mount up with wings as ea- gles, They will run____ and not be

wea- ry, They will walk, will walk and faint_ not. Those who

CD2:06

wait up- on the Lord will have strength.____ If the

trees nev- er blos- som, if no fruit is on the vine, If the

Softly and Tenderly

WILL L. THOMPSON

RAYMOND BROWN
Arr. by Doug Holck
Duet arr. by Tom Fettke

See on the por - tals He's wait - ing and watch - ing,
Why should we lin - ger and heed not His mer - cies,

See on the por - tals He's wait - ing and watch - ing,
Why should we lin - ger and heed not His mer - cies,

Watch - ing for you and for me._____ Come
Mer - cies for you and for me?_____

Watch - ing for you and for me._____
Mer - cies for you and for me?_____ Come__

home,_____ come__ home._____

Ye who are wea - ry, come home.

Ear - nest - ly, ten - der - ly Je - sus is call - ing,

CD2:10 *2nd time*

Call - ing, "O sin - ner, come home." home."

Voice II (or both voices unison)

Time is now fleet - ing; the mo - ments are pass - ing,

Pass - ing from you and from me.

Shad - ows are gath - 'ring, death's night is com - ing,

CD2:11 cresc. slight rit.

Com - ing for you and for me.

cresc. slight rit.

a tempo
f *Voice I*
Mel. *Voice II*
O for the won - der - ful love He has prom - ised,

f a tempo

Glorious Is Thy Name

includes

Glorious Is Thy Name (Mozart)

Glorious Is Thy Name (McKinney)

Arr. by Tom Fettke

98

28 *"Glorious Is Thy Name" (B. B. McKinney)

100

Your Love Compels Me

with

And Can It Be?

*Arr. by Tom Fettke
and Doug Holck*

104

The Lord Is My Light

Adapted from Psalm 27

FRANCES ALLITSEN
Arr. by William David Young
Duet arr. by Tom Fettke

host of men were laid _____ a - gainst me, Yet shall

not my heart be a - fraid; And though there

'rose up war a - gainst _____ me, _____

Yet will I put my trust in Him.

Worthy Is the Lamb

Adapted from
Revelation 5:12-13 by B. H.

BENJAMIN HARLAN
Duet arr. by Tom Fettke

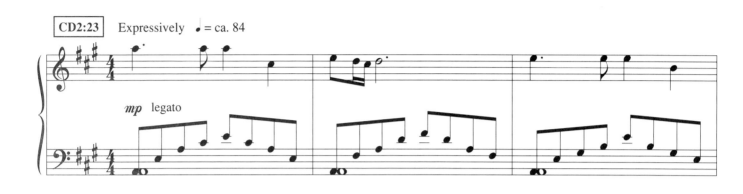

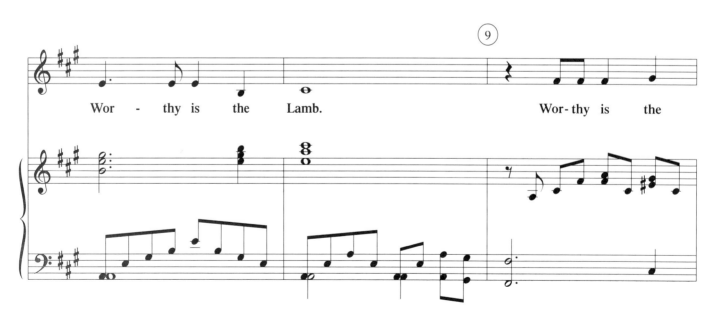

CD2:26

Come, Every One Who Is Thirsty

L. J. R.

LUCY J. RIDER
Arr. by Gene Thomas
and Tom Fettke

All that you're long - ing for. Come and be glad.
11
"I will pour wa - ter on him who is thirst - y; I will pour
mp
15
cresc.
Mel.
floods up - on the dry ground. O - pen your heart for the
cresc.
decresc.
gift I am bring - ing. While you are seek - ing Me
decresc.

124

Crown Him with Many Crowns

Stanzas 1 and 3: MATTHEW BRIDGES
Stanza 2: GODFREY THRING

GEORGE J. ELVEY
Arr. by O. D Hall, Jr.
Duet arr. by Tom Fettke
Piano transcription by Randy Smith

We Shall All Be Changed

1 Cor. 15:51, 52; I Thess. 4:17
Adapted by Tom Fettke and Bob Ashton

TOM FETTKE and BOB ASHTON

136

God Exalted Him

LINDA LEE JOHNSON
Based on Philippians 2:5-11

TOM FETTKE

140

names; That ev-'ry knee should bow in earth and heav'n a-bove,

And ev-'ry tongue con-fess that Je-sus Christ is Lord.

ff And ev-'ry tongue con-fess that Je-sus Christ is

rit. and dim.

Lord; He is Lord, He is Lord.

The Foundation

includes

The Solid Rock
The Church's One Foundation

Arr. by Tom Fettke

143

*"The Church's One Foundation" (Samuel Stone-Samuel Wesley)

Church-'s one foun-da-tion Is Je-sus Christ, her Lord. She

is His new cre-a-tion By wa-ter and the Word. From

heav'n He came and sought her To be His ho-ly

144